Meal time

AROUND THE WORLD

First published 1992 by UNICEF-UK/Bright Books Ltd

Text: by Barbara Kennett © UNICEF-UK

Illustrated borders/cover: by Colin Hollidge © UNICEF-UK

All rights reserved by UNICEF-UK

Typeset by Set Two, Ely, Cambridgeshire

Printed in Hong Kong by Wing King Tong

ISBN 1-873967-04-7

Every minute of
the day
Whether working,
or at play,
Someone somewhere
stops to say
"Is it mealtime?"

Turn the pages.
    Now, shall we
Look around the
    world and see
Breakfast, break time,
    dinner, tea
How others take
    their food.

Busy mother, as
  you see
Picking for her family
Someone's dreaming
  cosily
On her back.

Hurry, hurry – don't be late
Food is waiting on your plate!
Here is something that can't wait –
First we wash our hands!

Precious, for each
    son and daughter
Round the world, is
    good, clean water.
Walk with care, her
    mother taught her
Mustn't spill a drop.

Pumping water is my task
Work the handle – not too fast
Use with care and make it last.
See how strong I am!

Baby's sleeping in
   his bed
Children quiet –
   think ahead:
Time to make the
   family's bread
In the sunshine.

Cook by woodfire: there's a test!
Choose the sticks that burn the best
Carry, like some great bird's nest
Home on your head.

Add the flame and, one . . .two . . . three . . .
Stoves are burning merrily
'Thought perhaps you'd like to see
How we cook our food.

Do you like pancakes? So do we –
Called a different name, maybe,
Good and filling for our tea
What do you like with yours?

Stir your food and make a wish,
Something special in your dish
Fingers help when catching fish
My! They do taste good!

Cosy room: the log fire's gleaming
Food smells good, it's hot and steaming
Time for eating, not for dreaming –
Or else he'll eat yours too!

Feast-day bells ring out their chime
Happy mothers – busy time
Hope they won't forget that I'm
Peeping hungrily.

School bells too ring out their rhyme.
"Eat up children, dinner time!"
There's a place here, next to mine.
Won't you join us?

Tempting smells
   upon the air
Eager faces
   everywhere
Cooked with love,
   now, serve with care
To your friends.

Sharing lunch – but
please excuse,
Chopsticks are quite
hard to use
Won't be beaten:
we refuse
To lose one single bit!

How do you drink up your juice?
Half a gourd is what I use
Mummy tips, so I don't lose
Too much down my chin.

Juicy fruit will
   quench his thirst
Lucky him – he got
   there first
I'm so thirsty I could
   BURST!
Perhaps he'll share
   with me.

Food is finished –
off we race
Can't go out with
sticky face
Wash away each
tiny trace
Of our meal.

Mum is at the
  washroom door
Time for brushing
  teeth, once more,
Make them sparkle,
  ready for
Our next mealtime.

What is UNICEF?

UNICEF is the United Nations Children's Fund. It helps the world to keep its promises to children. We work in 128 of the world's poorest countries running low-cost long-term development programmes which help save the lives of over 4 million children every year and improve the lives of millions more. In addition to our long-term programmes UNICEF constantly responds to emergency situations around the world.

UNICEF's programmes include health, safe water, immunisation, nutrition and education, both for children and for their families. UNICEF works in partnership with governments, community organisations and local people, regardless of politics, religion, race or colour. The only criterion is need.

 Child health

 Local services for children and women

 Clean water supply and sanitation

 Formal and non-formal education

 Child nutrition

 Emergency relief

UNICEF in the UK

UNICEF is represented in this country by the UK Committee for UNICEF, one of 33 National Committees in the industrialised countries whose work is to raise funds for UNICEF programmes and to raise awareness of the needs of children. Seven regional offices support a nationwide network of local volunteer groups and individuals, who are the backbone of UNICEF-UK. Their contribution is vital because UNICEF depends entirely on voluntary donations to carry out its work.

UNICEF and you

How you can help:

If you and your family would like to know more about UNICEF, you can find out about local activities and about selling UNICEF greetings cards and products by writing to:

UNICEF-UK
55 Lincoln's Inn Fields
London WC2A 3NB.
Telephone: 071 405 5592

PHOTO CREDITS

Cover + pages 2/3 and 16/17: Colin Hollidge
Page 4: UNICEF Botswana: Carolyn Watson
Page 12: UNICEF Mexico City: Heather Jarvis
Page 18: UNICEF Ethiopia: Peter Magubani
All other photos: UNICEF library